To my wonderful family: Paul, Phyllis, Jane, Lisa, and Zac
—A. B.

This edition published in 1993 by SMITHMARK Publishers Inc.
16 East 32nd Street, New York, NY 10016

SMITHMARK books are available for bulk purchase for sales promotion and premium use.
For details write or call the manager of special sales, SMITHMARK Publishers Inc.
16 East 32nd Street, New York, NY 10016; (212) 532-6600.

Produced by RGA Publishing Group, Inc.
2029 Century Park East, Suite 3290
Los Angeles, CA 90067

ISBN: 0-8317-2530-3

Printed in the United States of America

10 9 8 7 6 5 4 3 2 1

THINKING GREEN
In My Home

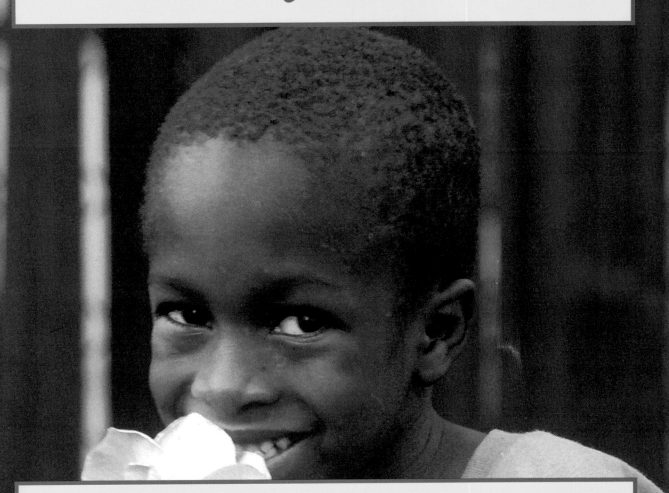

Photographs by Ann Bogart

Green is the color of grass and leaves. When we
"think green," it means we care about all
living things, including plants and animals.

There are lots of ways to "think green" right in our own home. We can start by remembering the "three R's"— **reduce**, **reuse**, **recycle**!

We can save newspapers. When we do, we **reduce** the number of trees that have to be cut down to make the newspapers.

It also means saving plastic bottles, **aluminum** cans, and glass jars so they can be *reused* or *recycled* into new **containers**.

To save electricity, we turn off the lights
when they're not needed.

To save water, we turn off the faucet between
brushing and rinsing our teeth.

We also save water when we wash our car by filling
a bucket instead of running the hose.

And when we use soap, we make sure it won't
harm animals or plants.

We can also "think green" by growing our own food in a vegetable garden.

Then we **recycle** the food we don't use by making **compost** from our table scraps. The **compost** will be used to **nourish** our garden!

To **conserve energy** in the winter, we wear sweaters indoors instead of turning up the heat.

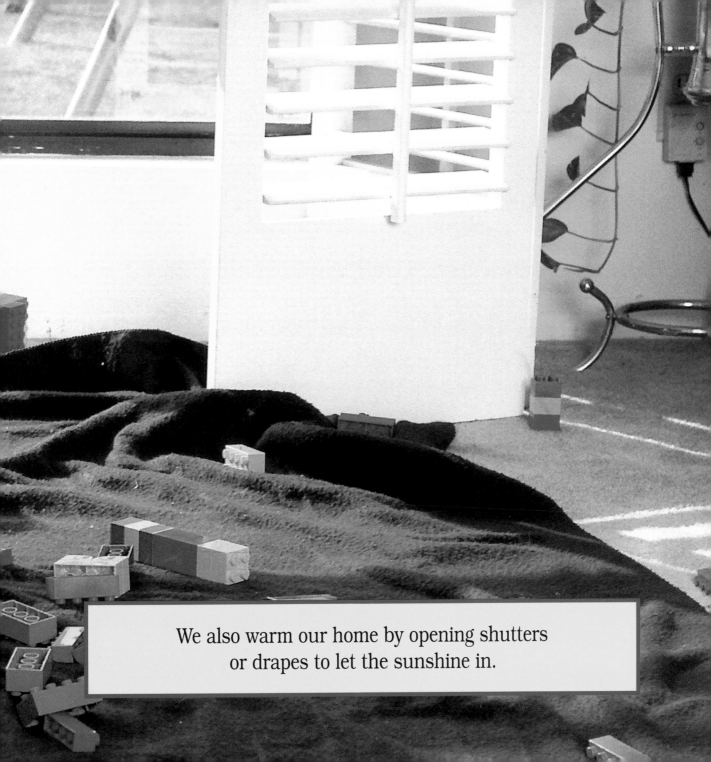

We also warm our home by opening shutters
or drapes to let the sunshine in.

In summer, we wear cool clothes so we don't have to use the air-conditioning, which wastes **energy.**

And we close our drapes or shutters to keep the sun from making the house too warm.

Instead of using paper towels that have to be
thrown away after one use, we dry our dishes
and our hands with cloth towels.

"Thinking green" can be fun! Why not invite your friends
over and show them how they can "think green," too!